Near this Site

WILLIAM PENN and WILLIAM MEAD

were tried in 1670

for preaching to an unlawful assembly
in Gracechurch Street

This Tablet Commemorates
the courage and endurance of the Jury Thos Vere Edward Bushell
and ten others, who refused to give a verdict against them although
locked up without food for two nights and were fined for their final
verdict of Not Guilty

The case of these Jurymen was reviewed in a Writ of Habeas Corpus
and Chief Justice Vaughan delivered the opinion of the court
which established The Right of Juries to give their Verdict
according to their Conscience.

The Trial of William Penn
and William Mead

at the Old Bailey,

1670.

Reprinted for the " Penn, Mead, and Jury Commemoration Committee," from the original 4to, issued in the Year 1670.

London: HEADLEY BROTHERS,
14, Bishopsgate Street Without, E.C.

HEADLEY BROTHERS,
PRINTERS, LONDON,
AND ASHFORD, KENT.

PREFATORY NOTE.

THE frontispiece of this volume represents the Tablet recently placed in the New Central Criminal Court, Newgate Street, London, close to the spot at the Old Bailey, where Penn and Mead were tried, in September 1670.

It was erected on the initiative of Horace J. Smith, of Philadelphia, and Moseley, Worcestershire, who did not, however, live to see it completed. A Committee was formed for the purpose, and consent was kindly given by the City Council for the inscription to be placed on a tablet in the Great Hall, on the ground floor of the building. The Committee who received subscriptions for the monument, also reprinted from the first edition, issued in 1670, this copy of the account of the trial, with the argument following, incorporating the errata, and a few obvious additions and corrections made in the second edition, published in the same year. A facsimile of the original title-page has been reproduced.

As regards the composition of the bench of magistrates who sat with Sir Samuel Sterling, the Lord Mayor, to try the case, four of them had already filled that office, viz., Sir Richard Browne in 1661 ; Sir John Robinson in 1663 ; Sir Thomas Bludworth in 1666 ; and Sir William Peake in 1668. The two other Aldermen, Sir Richard Ford and Sir Joseph Sheldon, were to become Lord Mayor of London in 1671, and 1676, respectively. One of the Sheriffs, Sir James Edwards, was Lord Mayor in 1679. Sir John Howell held the office of Recorder from 1668 to 1678.

JOHN HENRY LLOYD,
Chairman of the Committee.

Birmingham,
February, 1908.

THE
Peoples {Ancient and Juſt} Liberties
ASSERTED,

IN THE
TRYAL
OF

William Penn, and *William Mead*,

At the Seſſions held at the *Old-Baily* in *London*, the firſt, third, fourth and fifth of *Sept.* 70. againſt the moſt Arbitrary procedure of that Court.

Iſa. 10. 1, 2. *We unto them that Decree Unrighteous Decrees, and write grievonſneſs, which they have preſcribed ; to turn away the Needy from Judgment, and to take away the right from the Poor, &c.*

Pſal. 94. 20. *Shall the Throne of Iniquity have fellowſhip with thee, which frameth miſchief by a Law.*

Sic volo, ſic jubeo, ſtat pro ratione voluntas.

Old-Baily, 1ſt. 3d. 4th, 5th of *Sept.* 1670.

Printed in the Year, 1670,

To the English Reader.

IF ever it were time to speak, or write, tis now, so many strange Occurrances, requiring both.

How much thou art concerned in this ensuing Tryal (where not only the Prisoners, but the Fundamental Laws of England) have been most Arbitrarily Arraigned, Read, and thou mayst plainly judge.

Liberty of Conscience, is counted a Pretence for Rebellion, and Religious Assemblies, Routs, and Riots; and the Defenders of both, are by them, reputed Factious and disaffected.

Magna Charta, is Magnaf—with the Recorder of London; and to demand Right an affront to the Court.

Will and Power are their great Charter, but to call for Englands, is a Crime, incurring the penalty of their Bale-Dock, and Nasty-hole, nay, the menace of a Gag, and Iron Shackles too.

The Jury (though proper Judges) of Law and Fact) they would have over-ruled in both, as if their Verdict signified no more, then to eccho back the illegal charge of the Bench; and because their courage, and honesty did more then hold pace, with the threat and abuse of those, who sate as Judges, (after two dayes and two nights restraint for a Verdict) in the end were fined and imprisoned, for giving it.

O! what monstrous, and illegal proceedings are these? Who reasonably can call his Coat his own? When Property, is made subservient to the Will and Interest of his Judges; or, who can truly esteem himself a Free man? When all Pleas for liberty are esteemed Sedition, and the Laws, that give, and maintain them, so many insignificant pieces of formality.

And What do they less then plainly tell us so, who at will and pleasure, break open our Locks, rob our Houses, raze their Foundations, imprison our Persons, and finally deny us Justice *to our relief ; as if they then acted most like Christian men, when they were most barbarous, in ruining such as really are so ; and that no Sacrifice could be so acceptable to God, as the destruction of those, that most fear him.*

In short, That the Conscientious should only be obnoxious, and the just demand of our Religious Liberty, the reason why we should be denied our civil Freedom (as if to be a Christian and an English-man were inconsistant) and that so much solicitude and deep contrivance, should be imployed only to ensnare and ruin so many ten thousand consciencious Families) so eminently, industrious, serviceable and exemplary ; *whilst Murders can so easily obtain pardons, Rapes be remitted, publick Uncleanness pass unpunished, and all manner of* Levity, Prodigality, Excess, Prophaneness *and* Atheism, *universally connived at, (if not in some respect manifestly encouraged) cannot but be detestably abhorrent to every serious and honest mind.*

Yet that this lamentable state is true, and the present Project *in hand, let* London's Recorder, *and Canterburies* Chaplain *be heard.*

The first in his publick Panegerick, upon the Spanish Inquisition, highly admiring the prudence of the Romish Church, in the erection of it, as an excellent way, to prevent Schism, *which unhappy expression, at once passeth sentence, both against our fundamental Laws, and Protestant Reformation.*

The second, In his printed Mercenary discourse against Toleration, *asserting for a main Principle,* That it would be less injurious, to the Government, to dispence with prophane and loose Persons, then to allow a toleration to religious Dissenters : *It were to over-do the business, to say any more, where there is so much said already.*

And therefore to conclude, we cannot choose but admonish all, as well Persecutors, *to relinquish their Heady, Partial, and Inhumane Prosecutions (as what will certainly issue in disgrace here, and inevitable condign punishment hereafter) as those who yet dare express their moderation (however out of fashion, or made the brand of Phanatischism) not to be huf'd, or menaced, out of that excellent temper, to make their parts, and persons subservient to the base humors, and sinister designs of the biggest mortal upon Earth : But to reverence and obey, the Eternal just God,* before whose great Tribunal, all must render their accounts, and where he will recompence to every Person according to his works.

THE

The Tryal of William Penn and William Mead.

A S there can be no Observation, where there is no Action ; so its impossible, there should be a juditious Intelligence, without due Observation.

And since there can be nothing more seasonable then a right information, especially of *Publick Acts ;* and well knowing, how industrious some will be, to mis-represent, this Trial to the disadvantage of the Cause and Prisoners, it was thought requisite, in defence of both, and for the satisfaction of the People, to make it more publick ; nor can there be any business wherein the People of *England* are more concerned, then in that which relates to their civil and Religious Liberties, questioned in the Persons above named, at the *Old-Baily,* the first, third, fourth and fifth of *Sept.* 1670.

There being present on the Bench, as Justices.

Sam. Starling, Mayor,	*John Robinson,* Alderm.	
John Howel, Recorder.	*Joseph Shelden,* Alderm.	
Tho. Bludworth, Alder.	*Richard Brown,*	
William Peak, Alderm.	*John Smith,*	Sheriffs.
Richard Ford, Alderm.	*James Edwards,*	

The Citizens of *London* that were summoned for Jurors, appearing, were impannelled, *viz.*

Clar. Call over the Jury.

Cryer. O yes, *Thomas Veer, Edward* Bushel, John Hammond Charles Milson, Gregory Walklet, John Brightman, Wil. Plumsted, Hen. Henly, James† Damask, Henry Michel, William Lever, John Baily.*

---

* This is John in the first edition.   † Thomas.

The Form of the Oath.

You shall well and truely try, and true Deliverance make betwixt our Soveraign Lord the King, and the Prisoners at the Bar, according to your Evidence ; So help you God.

The Indictment.

That *William Penn*, Gent. and *Willam Mead* late of *London*, *Linnen-Draper*, with divers other Persons, to the Jurors unknown, to the number of three hundred, the 14th day of *August*, in the 22th year of the *King*, about eleaven of the clock in the forenoon, the same day, with Force and Arms, &c. in the Parish of St. *Bent Grace-Church* in *Bridge-ward*, *London*, in the street called *Gratious-Church-Street*, unlawfully and tumultuously did assemble and congregate themselves together, to the disturbance of the Peace of the said Lord the King : and the aforesaid *William Penn*, and *William Mead*, together with other Persons, to the Jurors aforesaid unknown, then and there so assembled and congregated together ; the aforesaid *William Penn*, by agreement between him and *William Mead*, before made ; and by abetment of the aforesaid *William Mead* then and there, in the open Street, did take upon himself to preach and speak, and then, and there, did preach and speak unto the aforesaid *William Mead*, and other Persons there, in the Street aforesaid, being assembled and congregated together, by reason whereof a great concourse and tumult of People in the Street aforesaid, then and there, along time did remain and continue, in contempt of the said Lord the King, and of his Law, to the great disturbance of his Peace, to the great terror and disturbance of many of his Liege people and Subjects, to the ill example of all others, in the like case Offenders, and against the Peace of the said *Lord the King*, his Crown and Dignity.

What say you, *William Penn* and *William Mead*, are you guilty, as you stand indicted, in manner and form, as aforesaid, or not guilty.

Penn, It is impossible, that we should be able to remember the Indictment verbatim, and therefore we desire a Copy of it, as is customary in the like occasions.

Rec. *You must first plead to the Indictment, before you can have a Copy of it.*

Pen. I am unacquainted with the formality of the Law, and therefore, before I shall answer directly, I request two things of the Court. First, that no advantage may be taken against me, nor I deprived of any benefit, which I might otherwise have received. Secondly, that you will promise me a fair hearing, and liberty of making my defence.

Court, No advantage shall be taken against you ; you shall have liberty, you shall be heard.

Pen. Then I plead not guilty in manner and form.

Cla. *What sayest thou*, William Mead, *art thou guilty in manner and form, as thou standest indicted, or not guilty ?*

Mead. I shall desire the same liberty as is promised *William Penn*.

Court, *You shall have it*.

Mead. Then I plead not guilty in manner and form.

The Court adjourned until the afternoon.

Cryer, O yes, &c.

Cla. *Bring* William Penn *and* William Mead *to the Bar*.

Obser. The said Prisoners were brought, but were set aside, and other business prosecuted. Where we cannot choose but observe, that it was the constant and unkind practices of the Court, to the Prisoners, to make them wait upon the Tryals of Fellons and Murderers, thereby designing in all probability, *both to affront and tire them*.

After five hours attendance, the Court broke up and adjourned to the third instant.

The third of *September*, 1670, the Court sate.

Cry, O yes, &c.

Cla. *Bring* William Penn *and* William Mead *to the Bar.*

Mayor, Sirrah, who bid you put off their Hats ? put on their Hats again.

Obser. Whereupon one of the Officers putting the Prisoners Hats upon their heads (pursuant to the Order of the Court) brought them to the Bar.

Record. Do you know where you are ?

Pen. Yes.

Record. Do not you know it is the Kings Court ?

Pen. I know it to be a Court, and I suppose it to be the Kings Court.

Record. Do you not know there is respect due to the Court ?

Pen. Yes.

Rec. Why do you not pay it then ?

Pen. I do so.

Rec. Why do you not pull off your Hat then ?

Pen. Because I do not believe that to be any respect.

Record. Well, the Court sets forty Marks apiece upon your Heads, as a Fine for your contempt of the Court.

Pen. I desire it might be observed, that we came into the Court with our Hats off, (that is, taken off) and if they have been put on since, it was by order from the Bench ; and therefore not we, but the Bench should be fined.

Mead, I have a Question to ask the *Recorder*, Am I fined also.

Recor. Yes.

Mead, I desire the Jury, and all people to take notice of this injustice of the *Recorder*, who spake not to me to pull

off my Hat, and yet hath he put a Fine upon my head. O
fear the Lord, and dread his Power, and yield to the guidance
of his holy Spirit ; for he is not far from everyone of you.

The *Jury* Sworn again.

Obser. J. *Robinson* Lievetenant of the *Tower*, disingeni-
ously objected against *Edw. Bushel*, as if he had not kist the
Book, and therefore would have him sworn again ; though
indeed, it was on purpose, to have made use of his tenderness
of Conscience in avoiding reiterated Oaths, to have put him
by his being a Jury-man, apprehending him to be a person,
not fit to Answer their arbitrary ends.

The Clark read the Indictment, as aforesaid,

Clar. Cryer, Call *James Cook* into the Court, give him
his Oath.

Cla. *James Cook* lay your hand upon the book, the
evidence you shall give to the Court, betwixt our Soveraign
the King, and the Prisoners at the Bar, shall be the Truth,
and the whole Truth, and nothing but the Truth ; so help
you God, &c.

*Cook. I was sent for, from the Exchange, to go and disperse a
Meeting in* Gratious-street, *where I saw Mr.* Penn *speaking
to the people, but I could not hear what he said, because of the
noise ; I endeavoured to make way to take him, but I could not
get to him for the crowd of people ; upon which Captain* Mead
*came to me, about the Kennel of the Street, and desired me
to let him go on ; for when he had done, he would bring Mr.*
Penn *to me.*

Court. What number do you think might be there ?

Cook. About three or four hundred people.

Court. Call Richard Read, *Give him his Oath.*

Read being sworn was askt, *What do you know concerning
the Prisoners at the Bar.*

Read, My Lord, I went to Gratious-street, *where I found a
great crowd of People, and I heard Mr.* Penn *preach to them ;*

and I saw Captain Mead *speaking to Lievtenant* Cook, *but what he said, I could not tell.*

Mead. What did *William Penn* say?

Read. There was such a great noise, that I could not tell what he said.

Mead. Jury, observe this Evidence, he saith he heard him preach, and yet saith, he doth not know what he said.

Jury take notice, he swears now a clean contrary thing, to what he swore before the Mayor, when we were committed: For now he swears that he saw me in *Gratious-street*, and yet swore before the *Mayor*, when I was committed, that he did not see me there. I appeal to the Mayor himself, if this be not true; but no answer was given.

Cour. *What number do you think might be there?*

Read. *About four or five hundred.*

Pen. I desire to know of him what day it was?

Read. The 14th day of *August.*

Pen. Did he speak to me, or let me know he was there; for I am very sure I never saw him.

Cla. Cryer, *Call—— ——into the Court.*

Cour. *Give him his Oath.*

My Lord, I saw a great number of People, and Mr. Penn, *I suppose was speaking; I see him make a motion with his hands, and heard some noise, but could not understand what he said; but for Captain* Mead, *I did not see him there.*

Rec. What say you *Mr. Mead?* Were you there?

Mead. It is a Maxim in your own Law, *Nemo tenetur accusare seipsum,* which if it be not true Latine, I am sure it is true English, *That no man is bound to accuse himself:* And why dost thou offer to ensnare me, with such a question? Doth not this shew thy malice? Is this like unto a Judge, that ought to be Counsel for the Prisoner at the Bar?

Record. Sir, Hold your Tongue, I did not go about to en-snare you.

Pen. I desire we may come more close to the point, and that silence be commanded in the Court.

Cry. O yes, All manner of Persons keep silence upon pain of imprisonment———Silence in the Court.

Pen. We confess our selves to be so far from recanting, or declining to vindicate the assembling of our selves, to Preach, Pray, or Worship the Eternal, Holy, Just God, that we declare to all the World, that we do believe it to be our indispensable duty, to meet incessantly upon so good an account ; nor shall all the powers upon Earth, be able to divert us from reverencing and adoring our God, who made us.

Brown. You are not here for worshipping God, but for breaking the Law ; you do yourselves a great deal of wrong in going on in that discourse.

Pen. I affirm I have broken no Law, nor am I guilty of the Indictment, that is laid to my charge, and to the end the Bench, the Jury, and myself, with these that hear us, may have a most direct understanding of this procedure, I desire you would let me know by what Law it is you prosecute me, and upon what Law you ground my indictment.

Rec. Upon the Common-Law.

Pen. Where is that Common-Law ?

Rec. You must not think that I am able to run up so many years, and over so many adjudged Cases, which we call Common-Law, to answer your curiosity.

Pen. This Answer I am sure is very short of my Question, for if it be Common, it should not be so hard to produce.

Rec. Sir, will you plead to your Indictment ?

Pen. Shall I plead to an Indictment, that hath no Foundation in Law, if it contain that Law you say I have broken, why should you decline to produce that Law, since it will be imposible for the *Jury* to determine, or agree to bring in their Verdict, who have not the Law produced by which they should measure the truth of this Indictment, and the guilt, or contrary, of my fact?

Rec. *You are a saucy Fellow, speak to the Indictment.*

Pen. I say, it is my place to speak to matter of Law; I am arraigned a Prisoner, my liberty, which is next to life it self, is now concerned; you are many Mouths and Ears against me, and if I must not *Obser. At this time several upon the Bench urged hard upon the Prisoner to bear him down.* be allowed to make the best of my Case, it is hard: I say again, unless you shew me, and the People, the Law you ground your Indictment upon; I shall take it for granted, your proceedings are meerly Arbitrary.

Rec. *The Question is whether you are guilty of this Indictment?*

Pen. The Question is not whether I am guilty of this Indictment, but whether this Indictment be legal, it is too general and imperfect an Answer, to say it is the Common Law, unless we knew both where, and what it is; For where there is no Law, there is no Transgression; and that Law which is not in being, is so far from being Common, that it is no Law at all.

Rec. *You are an impertinent Fellow, Will you teach the Court what Law is? Its* Lex non scripta, *that which many have studied thirty or forty years to know, and would you have me to tell you in a moment?*

Pen. Certainly, If the Common Law be so hard to be understood, its far from being very Common; but if the Lord *Cook* in his Institutes, be of any consideration, he tells us, That Common Law is Common Right, and that Common Right is the great Charter-Priviledges: Confirmed 9 *Hen.* 3. 29. 25 *Edw.* 1. 1. 2. *Edw.* 3. 8. *Cook Inst.* 2. p. 56.

Rec. *Sir, you are a troublesom Fellow, and it is not for the honour of the Court to suffer you to go on.*

Pen. I have asked but one Question, and you have not answered me ; though the Rights and Priviledges of every Englishman be concerned in it.

Rec. *If I should suffer you to ask Questions till to morrow morning you would be never the wiser.*

Pen. That is according as the Answers are.

Rec. *Sir, We must not stand to hear you talk all night.*

Pen. I design no affront to the Court, but to be heard in my just Plea ; and I must plainly tell you, that if you will deny me *Oyer* of that Law, which you suggest I have broken, you do at once deny me an acknowledged right, and evidence to the whole World your resolution to sacrifice the Priviledges of Englishmen, to your Sinister and Arbitrary designs.

Rec. *Take him away : My Lord, if you take not some course with this pestilent Fellow, to stop his Mouth, we shall not be able to do any thing to Night.*

May. *Take him away, Take him away, turn him into the Bale-dock.*

Pen. These are but so many vain Exclamations ; Is this Justice or true Judgment ? Must I therefore be taken away because I plead for the fundamental Laws of *England* ? However, this I leave upon your Consciences, who are of the Jury (and my sole Judges) that if these Antient Fundamental Laws, which relate to liberty and property, and (are not limited to particular perswasions in matters of Religion) must not be indispensibly maintained and observed ; Who can say he hath right to the Coat upon his back ? Certainly our liberties are openly to be invaded, our Wives to be ravished, our Children slaved, our Families ruined, and our Estates led away in Triumph, by every sturdy Beggar and Malicious Informer, as their Trophies, but our (pretended) Forfeits for Conscience sake ; the Lord of Heaven and Earth will be Judge between us in this matter.

Rec. *Be silent there.*

Pen. I am not to be silent in a Case wherein I am so much concerned, and not only my self, but many ten thousand Families besides.

Obser. They having rudely haled him into the Bale-dock, *William Mead* they left in Court, who spake as followeth.

Mead, You men of the Jury, here I do now stand, to answer to an Indictment against me, which is a bundle of Stuff, full of Lyes and Falshoods ; for therein I am accused, that I met *vi et armis, illicite et tumultuose :* time was, when I had freedom to use a carnal Weapon, and then I thought I feared no man ; but now I fear the Living God, and dare not make use thereof, nor hurt any man ; nor do I know I demeaned my self as a tumultuous person. I say, I am a peaceable man, therefore it is a very proper Question what *William Penn* demanded in this Case, An *OYER* of the Law, on which our Indictment is grounded.

Rec. *I have made answer to that already.*

Mead, Turning his face to the Jury, said, You men of the Jury, who are my Judges, if the *Recorder* will not tell you what makes a Riot, a Rout, or an unlawful Assembly, *Cook,* he that once they called the Lord *Cook,* tells us what makes a Riot, a Rout, and an unlawfull Assembly——A Riot is when three, or more, are met together to beat a man, or to enter forcibly into another mans Land, to cut down his Grass, his Wood, or break down his Pales.

Obser. Here the *Recorder* interrupted him, and said, I thank you Sir, that you will tell me what the Law is, scornfully pulling off his Hat.

Mead, Thou mayst put on thy Hat, I have never a Fee for thee now.

Brown, He talkes at random, one while an Independent,

another while some other Religion, and now a Quaker, *and next a* Papist.

Mead. Turpe est doctorum cum culpa redarguit ad ipsum.

May. You deserve to have your Tongue cut out.

Rec. If you discourse on this manner, I shall take occasion against you.

Mead, Thou didst promise me, I should have fair Liberty to be heard. Why may I not have the Priviledge of an Englishman ? I am an Englishman, and you might be ashamed of this dealing.

Rec. I look upon you to be an Enemy to the Laws of England, *which ought to be observed and kept, nor are you worthy of such Priviledges as others have.*

Mead, The Lord is Judge between me and thee in this matter.

Obser. Upon which they took him away into the Bale-dock, and the Recorder proceeded to give the Jury their charge, as followeth.

Rec. You have heard what the Indictment is, It is for preaching to the People, and drawing a tumultuous Company after them and Mr. *Penn* was speaking ; if they should not be disturbed, you see they will go on ; there are three or four Witnesses, that have proved this, that he did preach there, that Mr. *Mead* did allow of it ; after this, you have heard by substantial Witnesses what is said against them : Now we are upon the Matter of fact, which you are to keep to, and observe, as what hath been fully sworn at your peril.

Obser. The Prisoners were put out of the Court, into the Bale-dock, and the charge given to the Jury in their absence, at which *W. P.* with a very raised Voice, it being a considerable distance from the Bench, spake.

Pen. I appeal to the Jury, who are my Judges, and this great Assembly, whether the proceedings of the Court are not most arbitrary, and void of all Law, in offering to give the Jury their Charge in the absence of the Prisoners ; I say, it is directly opposit to, and destructive of, the undoubted right of every English Prisoner, as *Cook* in the 2 *Inst.* 29 on the Chap. of *Magna Charta* speaks.

Obser. The Recorder being thus unexpectedly lasht for his extra-juditial proceedure, said with an inraged smile.

Rec. Why, ye are present, you do hear, do you not ?

Pen. No thanks to the Court, that commanded me into the Bale-dock ; and you of the Jury take notice, that I have not been heard, neither can you legally depart the Court, before I have been fully heard, having at least ten or twelve material points to offer, in order to invallid their Indictment.

Rec. Pull that Fellow down, pull him down.

Mead. Are these according to the rights and priviledges of Englishmen, that we should not be heard, but turned into the Bale-dock, for making our defence, and the Jury to have their Charge given them in our absence ; I say these are barbarous and unjust proceedings.

Rec. Take them away into the Hole; to hear them talk, all Night, as they would, that I think doth not become the honour of the Court; and I think you (i.e. the Jury) *your selves would be tired out, and not have patience to hear them.*

Obser. The *Jury* were commanded up to agree upon their verdict, the Prisoners remaining in the stinking Hole ; after an hour and halfs time eight came down agreed, but four remained above, the Court sent an Officer for them, and they accordingly came down : The Bench used many unworthy Threats to the four that dissented ; and the Recorder, addressing himself to *Bushel*, said, " Sir, You are the cause of " this disturbance, and manifestly shew your self an abettor " of faction, I shall set a Mark upon you Sir.

J. Robinson. Mr. *Bushel*, I have known you near this fourteen years ; you have thrust your self upon this Jury, because you think there is some service for you ; I tell you, you deserve to be indicted more then any man that hath been brought to the Bar this day.

Bush. No Sir *John*. There were threescore before me, and I would willingly have got off, but could not.

Bloodw. I said when I saw Mr. *Bushel*, what I see is come to pass, for I knew he would never yield. Mr. *Bushel*, we know what you are.

May. Sirrah, you are an impudent Fellow, I will put a Mark upon you.

Obser. They used much menacing Language, and be- haved themselves very imperiously to the Jury, as persons not more void of Justice then sober Education : after this barbarous usage, they sent them to consider of bringing in their Verdict, and after some considerable time they returned to the Court. Silence was called for, and the *Jury* called by their names.

Cla. Are you agreed upon your Verdict ?

Jury. Yes.

Cla. Who shall speak for you ?

Jury. Our Fore-man.

Cla. Look upon the Prisoners at the Bar ; How say you ? Is William Penn *guilty of the matter whereof he stands indicted in manner and form, or not guilty ?*

Fore-m. Guilty of Speaking in *Gratious-street.*

Court. Is that all ?

Fore-m. That is all I have in commission.

4

Recor. You had as good say nothing.

May. Was it not an unlawful Assembly ? you mean he was speaking to a Tumult of People there ?

Fore-m. My Lord, This was all I had in Commission.

Obser. Here some of the *Jury* seemed to buckle to the questions of the Court, upon which *Bushel, Hammond,* and some others opposed themselves, and said, they allowed of no such word, as an unlawful Assembly in their Verdict ; at which the *Recorder, Mayor, Robinson,* and *Bloodworth* took great occasion to villifie them with most approbious language ; and this Verdict not serving their turns, the *Recorder* expressed himself thus.

Recor. The Law of *England* will not allow you to depart till you have given in your Verdict.

Jury. We have given in our Verdict, and we can give in no other.

Recor. Gentlemen, you have not given in your Verdict, and you had as good say nothing ; therefore go and consider it once more, that we may make an end of this troublesome business.

Jury. We desire we may have Pen, Ink, and Paper.

Obser. The Court adjourned for half an hour ; which being expired, the Court returns, and the *Jury* not long after.

The Prisoners were brought to the Bar, and the *Juries* names called over.

Clar. Are you agreed of your Verdict ?

Jur. Yes.

Clar. Who shall speak for you ?

Jur. Our Fore-man.

Clar. What say you ? look upon the Prisoners ; Is *William Penn* guilty in Manner and Form, as he stands indicted, or not guilty ?

For-m. Here is our Verdict, holding forth a piece of Paper to the Clark of the Peace, which follows.

WE the *Jurors*, hereafter named, do find *William Penn* to be guilty of Speaking or Preaching to on Assembly, met together in *Gratious-Street*, the 14th of *August* last 1670. and that *William Mead* is not guilty of the said Indictment.

Fore-m.	*Thomas Veer,*	*Charles Milson,*
	Edward Bushel,	*Gregory Walklet,*
	John Hammond,	*John Baily,*
	Henry Henley,	*William Lever,*
	Henry Michel,	*James Damask,*
	John Brightman,	*Wil. Plumsted.*

Obser. This both *Mayor* and *Recorder* resented at so high a rate, that they exceeded the bounds of all reason and civility.

May. What! will you be lead by such a silly Fellow as *Bushel?* an impudent canting Fellow; I warrant you, you shall come no more upon Juries in haste: You are a Foreman indeed, addressing himself to the Fore-man, I thought you had understood your place better.

Rec. Gentlemen, You shall not be dismist till we have a Verdict, that the Court will accept; and you shall be lockt up, without Meat, Drink, Fire, and Tobacco; you shall not think thus to abuse the Court, we will have a Verdict, by the help of God, or you shall starve for it.

Pen. My Jury, who are my Judges, ought not to be thus menaced; their Verdict should be free, and not compelled; the Bench ought to wait upon them, but not forestaul them; I do desire that Justice may be done me, and that the arbitrary resolves of the Bench may not be made the measure of my Juries verdict.

Rec. Stop that prateing Fellows mouth, or put him out of the Court.

May. You have heard that he preacht, that he gathered a company of tumultuous people, and that they do not only disobey the martial Power, but civil also.

Pen. It is a great mistake, we did not make the tumult, but they that interrupted us ; the Jury cannot be so ignorant, as to think, that we met there, with a design to disturb the civil Peace, since (1st.) we were by force of Arms kept out of our Lawful House, and met as near it in the street, as their Souldiers, would give us leave ; and (2d.) because it was no new thing, (nor with the circumstances exprest in the indictment) but what was usual and customary with us ; tis very well known that we are a peaceable People, and cannot offer violence to any man.

Obser. The Court being ready to break up, and willing to huddle the Prisoners to their Goal, and the Jury to their chamber, *Penn* spoke as follows.

Pen. The agreement of twelve men is a Verdict in Law, and such a one being given by the Jury, *I require the Clark of the Peace to record it, as he will answer it, at his peril.* And if the *Jury* bring in another Verdict, contradictory to this, I affirm they are perjured men in Law. (and looking upon the *Jury* said) You are Englishmen, mind your Priviledge, give not away your Right.

Bush. &c. Nor will we ever do it.

Obser. One of the *Jury* men pleaded indisposition of body, and therefore desired to be dismist.

May. You are as strong as any of them ; starve them ; and hold your Principles.

Rec. Gentlemen, You must be contented with your hard fate, let your patience overcome it ; for the Court is resolved to have a Verdict, and that before you can be dismist.

Jury. We are agreed, we are agreed, we are agreed.

Obser. The Court swore several persons, to keep the *Iury* all night without Meat, Drink, Fire, or any other accommodation ; they had not so much as a Chamber-pot, though desired.

Cry. O yes, &c.

Obser. The Court adjourns till seven of the Clock next morning (being the fourth instant, vulgarly called Sunday) at which time the Prisoners were brought to the Bar; the Court sate, and the *Jury* called to bring in their Verdict.

Cry, O yes, &c.————Silence in the Court, upon pain of imprisonment.

The *Juries* names called over.

Cla. Are you agreed upon your Verdict ?

Jur. Yes.

Cla. Who shall speak for you ?

Jur. Our Fore-man

Cla. What say you ? look upon the Prisoners at the Bar ; Is *W. Penn* guilty of the matter whereof he stands indicted, in manner and form as aforesaid, or not guilty ?

Fore-man. *William Penn* is guilty of speaking in *Gratious-street.*

May. To an unlawful Assembly ?

Bush. No my Lord, We give no other Verdict then what we gave last night, we have no other Verdict to give.

May. You are a factious Fellow, I'le take a course with you.

Bloodw. I knew Mr. *Bushel* would not yield.

Bush. Sir *Tho.* I have done according to my Conscience.

May. That Conscience of yours would cut my throat.

Bush. No my Lord, it never shall.

May. But I will cut yours so soon as I can.

Rec. He has inspired the *Jury*, he has the spirit of Divination, methinks I feel him ; I will have a positive Verdict, or you shall starve for it.

Pen. I desire to ask the Recorder one Question ; Do you allow of the Verdict given of *William Mead* ?

Rec. It cannot be a Verdict, because you were indicted for a Conspiracy, and one being found not guilty, and not the other, it could not be a Verdict.

Pen. If *Not guilty* be not a Verdict, then you make of the *Jury* and *Magna Charta* but a meer Nose of Wax.

Mead, How ! is *Not guilty* no Verdict.

Rec. No, tis no Verdict.

Pen. I affirm that the consent of a *Jury,* is a Verdict in Law ; and if *W. M.* be not guilty, it consequently follows, that I am clear, since you have indicted us of a Conspiracy, and I could not possibly conspire alone.

Obser. There were many Passages, that could not be taken, which past between the *Jury* and the Court. The Jury went up again, having received a fresh charge from the Bench, if possible to extort an unjust verdict.

Cry. O yes, &c.—Silence in the Court.

Cour. Call over the *Jury.* Which was done.

Cla. What say you ? Is *William Penn* guilty of the matter whereof he stands indicted, in manner and form aforesaid, or not guilty.

Fore-man. Guilty of speaking in *Gratious-street.*

Rec. What is this to the purpose ? I say, I will have a verdict. And speaking to *Edw. Bushel* said, You are a factious Fellow ; I will set a Mark upon you ; and whilst I have any thing to do in the City, I will have an eye upon you.

May. Have you no more wit then to be led by such a pittiful Fellow ? I will cut his Nose.

Pen. It is intolerable that my Jury should be thus menaced ; Is this according to the fundamental Laws ? Are not they my proper Judges by the great Charter of *England ?* What hope is there of ever having justice done, when Juries are threatned, and their Verdicts rejected ? I am concerned to speak and grieved to see such arbitrary proceedings. *Did not the Lievtenant of the* Tower *render one of them worse then a Fellon ?* And do you not plainly seem to condemn such for factious Fellows, who answer not your ends ? Unhappy are those Juries, who are threatned to be fined, and starved, and ruined, if they give not in Verdicts contrary to their Consciences.

Rec. My Lord, you must take a course with that same Fellow.

May. Stop his Mouth; Jaylor bring Fetters, and stake him to the ground.

Pen. Do your pleasure, I matter not your Fetters.

Rec. Till now I never understood the reason of the policy and prudence of the Spaniards, *in suffering the Inquisition among them : And certainly it will never be well with us, till something like the Spanish Inquisition be in* England.

Obser. The Jury being required to go together to find another verdict and steadfastly refusing it (saying they could give no other Verdict, then what was already given) the Recorder in great passion was running off the Bench, with these words in his mouth, " I protest, I will sit here no longer " to hear these things. At which the Mayor calling, Stay, stay, he returned, and directed himself unto the Jury, and spoke as followeth.

Rec. Gentlemen, we shall not be at this Trade alwayes with you ; you will find the next Sessions of Parliament, there will be a Law made, that those that will not conform shall not have the protection of the Law. Mr. Lee, *draw up another Verdict, that they may bring it in special.*

Lee, I cannot tell how to do it.

Jur. We ought not to be returned, having all agreed, and set our hands to the Verdict.

Rec. Vour Verdict is nothing, you play upon the Court ; I say you shall go together, and bring in another Verdict, or you shall starve ; and I will have you carted about the City, as in Edward *the thirds time.*

Fore-m. We have given in our verdict, and all agreed to it, and if we give in another,it will be a force upon us to save our lives.

May. Take them up.

Offic. My Lord, they will not go up.

Obser. The Mayor spoke to the Sheriff, and he came off his seat, and said.

Sher. Come Gentlemen, you must go up ; you see I am commanded to make you go.

Obser. Upon which the *Jury* went up ; and several sworn, to keep them without any accommodation as aforesaid, till they brought in their verdict.

Cry. O yes, &c. The Court adjourns till to morrow morning at seven of the clock.

Obser. The Prisoners were remanded to New-Gate, where they remained till next morning, and then were brought unto the Court, which being sate, they proceeded as followeth.

Cry. O yes, &c.——Silence in the Court upon pain of imprisonment.

Cla. Set *William Penn* and *William Mead* to the Bar. Gentlemen of the *Jury*, answer to your Names, *Tho. Veer, Edw. Bushel, John Hammond, Henry Henly, Henry Michell, John Brightman, Charles Milson, Gregory Walklet, John Baily, William Leaver, James Damask, William Plumstead.* Are you all agreed of your Verdict ?

Jur. Yes.

Cla. Who shall speak for you ?

Iury. Our Fore-man.

Cla. Look upon the Prisoners. What say you ? is *William Penn* guilty of the matter whereof he stands indicted, in manner and form, &c. or not guilty ?

Fore-man. You have there read already our Verdict in writing, and our hands subscribed.

Obser. The Clark had the Paper, but was stopt by the

Recorder from reading of it ; and he commanded to ask for a positive verdict.

Fore-m. If you will not accept of it, I desire to have it back again.

Court. That Paper was no Verdict, and there shall be no advantage taken against you by it.

Cla. How say you, Is *William Penn* guilty, &c. or not guilty ?

Fore-m. Not guilty.

Cla. How say you ? Is *William Mead* guilty, &c. or not guilty ?

Fore-m. Not guilty.

Cla. Then hearken to your Verdict, you say, that *William Penn* is not guilty in manner and form as he stands indicted, you say that *William Mead* is not guilty in manner and form as he stands indicted, and so you say all.

Iury. Yes, we do so.

Obser. The Bench being unsatisfied with the verdict, commanded that every Person should distinctly answer to their names, and give in their verdict, which they unanimously did, in saying, *Not guilty*, to the great satisfaction of the Assembly.

Recorder. I am sorry, Gentlemen, you have followed your own judgments and Opinions, rather then the good and wholesom advice, which was given you ; God keep my life out of your hands ; but for this the Court fines you forty Marks a man ; and imprisonment till paid. At which *Penn* stept up towards the Bench, and said.

Pen. I demand my liberty, being freed by the Jury.

May. No, you are in for your Fines.

Pen. Fines, for what ?

May. For contempt of the Court.

Pen. I ask, if it be according to the fundamental Laws of *England*, that any English-man should be fined or amerced but by the judgment of his Peers or Jury ; since it expressly contradicts the fourteenth and twenty-ninth Chap. of the great Charter of *England*, which say, No Free-man ought to be amerced, but by the Oath of good and Lawful men of the Vicinage.

Rec. *Take him away, Take him away, take him out of the Court.*

Pen. I can never urge the fundamental Laws of *England*, but you cry, Take him away, take him away. But it is no wonder, *Since the Spanish-Inquisition hath so great a place in the Recorders heart.* God Almighty, who is just, will judge you all for these things.

Obser. They haled the Prisoners into the Bale-dock, and from thence sent them to New-Gate, for non payment of their Fines ; and so were their *Jury*.

An Appendix, *by way of* Defence *for the* Prisoners, *as what might have been offered against the Indictment, and illegal Proceedings of the Court thereon, had they not violently over-rul'd and stopp'd them.*

U Pon a sober disquisition into the several parts of the Indictment, we find it so wretchedly defective, as if it were nothing else but a meer composition of error, rather calculated to the malitious designs of the Judges, then to the least verity of fact committed by the Prisoners.

To prove this, what we say, will be a main help to discover the Arbitrary proceedings of the Bench in their frequent Menaces to the *Jury* ; as if it were not so much their Business to try, as to condemn the Prisoners ; and that not so much for any Fact they had committed, as what the Court would have suggested to the *Jury* to have been their Fact.

§. 1. *It is the constant Common Law of* England, *that no man should be Taken, Imprisoned, Amerced, Deseized of his Free-hold, of his Liberties or free Customs, but by the judgement of his Peers, which are vulgarly called a Jury, from* Jurare, *because they are sworn to do right.*

§. 2. The only assistance that is given the *Jury*, in order to a Verdict, is,

First, The *Evidence* given of the Fact committed, by the person indicted.

Secondly, The knowledge of that Law, Act or Statute the Indictment is grounded upon, and which the Prisoners are said to have transgressed.

§. 3. We shall neglect to mention here, how much they were deprived, of that just advantage the ancient equal Laws of *England* do allow ; designing it for a conclusion of the whole, and shall only speak here to matter of Fact and Law.

§. 4. The Evidence, you have read in the Tryal, the utmost import of which, is more then this, That *William Penn* was speaking in *Gratious-street*, to an Assembly of people, but knew not what he said, which is so great a Contradiction, as he that runs may read it ; for no man can say another man Preaches, and yet understand not what he saith ; he may conjecture it, but that is a lame evidence in Law, it might as well have been sworn, That he was speaking of Law, Physick, Trade, or any other matter of civil concernment. Besides there is no Law against Preaching what is Truth, whether it be in the Street, or in any other place ; nor is it possible, that any man can truly swear, That he Preacht Sedition, Heresie, &c. unless he so heard him, that he could tell what he said.

§. 5. The Evidence further saith, That *W. Mead* was there, *but till being in Gratious-street be a fault, and hearing a man speak the Witness knows not what, be contrary to Law,* the whole Evidence is useless and impertinent ; but what they want of that, they endeavour to supply with Indictment ; whose parts we proceed to consider.

Exceptions Against the Indictment.

§. 6. It saith, That the Prisoners [*were met upon the 15th day of* August, 1670] whereas their own Evidence affirms it to be upon the 14th day of *August*, 70.

§. 7. [*That they met with force and Arms*] which is so
great a Lye, that the Court had no better cover for it, then
to tell the Jury, it was only a piece of Form, urging that the
man tried for clipping of money this present Sessions had
the same words used in his indictment.

But that this Answer is too scanty, as well as it was too
weak to prevail with the Jury ; we desire it may be con-
sidered, that the same words may be used more of course,
and out of form at one time, then at another : And though
we grant they can have little force with any Jury in a Clippers
case, for meer Clipping ; yet they are words that give so just
a ground of jealousie, nay, that carry so clear an Evidence
of illegallity, where they are truly proved and affirmed
of any Meeting, as that they are the proper Roots, from
whence do spring those Branches which render an Indictment terrible, and an Assembly truly to the terror of the
people.

§. 8. [*Unlawfully, and tumultuously to disturb the Peace*]
which is as true, as what is said before, (that is, as false) this
will evidently appear to all that consider how lawful it is to
assemble, with no other design then to worship God, and
their calling a lawful Assembly an unlawfull one, no more
makes it so, then to say Light is Darkness, black is white,
concludes so impudent a falsity true.

In short, because to worship God can never be a crime,
no Meeting or Assembly, designing to worship God, can be
unlawfull. Such as go about to prove an unlawfull Assembly,
must prove the Assemblers intent not to Worship God, but
that no man can do, because no man can know another mans
intentions, and therefore its impossible that any should prove
such an Assembly unlawful. That is properly an unlawful
Assembly, according to the definition of the Law, when several
persons are met together, with design to use violence, and to
do mischief, but that Dissenters meet with no such intention,

is manifest to the whole World, therefore their Assemblies are not unlawful ; he that hath only right to be worshipped, which is God, hath only right to institute how he will be worshipped ; and such as worship him in that Way they apprehend him to have instituted, are so far from being unlawful Assemblies, that therein they do but express the duty they owe to God.

[*Tumultuously*] Imports as much as Disorderly, or an Assembly full of Noise, Busle, and Confusion, using force and violence, to the injury of Persons, Houses, or Grounds. But whether Religious Dissenters, in their peaceable Meetings, therein desiring and seeking nothing more then to express that duty they owe to God Almighty, be a Tumultuous action or meeting in the sence exprest (and which is the very definition of the Law) will be the question. Certainly such as call these Meetings tumultuous, and to break the peace, offer the greatest violence to common words, that can be well imagined ; for they may as rightly say, such persons meet adulterously, thievishly, &c. as to affirm they meet tumultuously, because they are as truly applicable ; in short, such particulars, as are required to prove them such Meetings in Law, are wholly wanting.

§. 9. [*To the disturbance of the peace.*]
If the disturbance of the peace be but matter of form with the rest, as is usually pleaded ; leave out this matter of form and then see what great matter will be left.

Certainly such Assemblies, as are not to the breach and disturbance of the peace, are far from being unlawful or tumultuary : but if the peace be broken by them, how comes it the evidence was so short ? We cannot believe it was in favour of the Prisoners. This may shew to all the reasonable World, how forward some are, to brand innocency with hateful Names, to bring a suspition, where there was none deserved.

§. 10 [*That the said* Penn *and* Mead *met by agreement before hand made.*]

But if persons that never saw each other, nor converse together, neither had correspondence by any other hand, cannot be said to be agreed, to any action, before it be done ; Then the Prisoners were far from an Agreement ; for they had never Seen, Converst nor Corresponded, directly, nor indirectly, before the Officers came to disturb the Assembly : We well know how far they would have stretch the word, *Agreement* or *Conspiracy ;* but God who brings to nought, the Counsels of the wicked, prevented their cruel designs.

§. 11. [*That* William Mead *did abet the said* William Penn *in preaching.*]

No man can be said to abet another, whilst they are both unknown to each other, especially in this case, where abetting follows agreeing, and agreeing supposes fore-knowledge. Nay the word abet in Law signifies to *command, procure or counsel* a person, which *W. Mead* could not be said to do, in reference to *W. Penn*, they being so great Strangers one to another, and at so great a distance ; for the Evidence proves that he was with Lievtenant *Cook*, and Lievtenant *Cook* swears he could not make his way to *W. Penn*, for the Croud.

§. 12. [*That* W. Penn's *preaching and speaking caused a great concourse and tumult of People to remain and continue a long time in the street.*]

But this is so improbable to believe, that the very nature of a Tumult admits of no such thing as preaching ; but implies a disorderly multitude, where all may be said to speak, rather then any to hear.

§. 1. [*In contempt of the King and his Laws.*]

They are so far from contemning the King and his Laws, that they are obleiged and constrained by their own principles, to obey every Ordinance of man for the Lords sake, *but not against the Lord for mans sake,* which is the question in hand. Besides, their continuance there, was not in contempt, but by the permission of the chief Officer present, that came there by the Kings authority ; nor is it for the honour of the King that such persons should be said to act in contempt of his Laws, as only meet to honour God and his Laws.

§. 2. [*And to the great disturbance of the Kings Peace.*]

It is far from disturbing and breaking the Kings Peace, for men peaceably to meet to worship God ; for it is then properly broken and invaded, when force and violence are used, to the hurt and prejudice of Persons and Estates ; or when anything is done that tends to the stirring up of Sedition, and begetting in people a dislike of the Civil Government : But that such things are not practised by us in our Assemblies, either to offer violence to mens Persons and Estates, or to stir up People to Sedition, or dislike to the civil Government, is obvious to all that visit our Assemblies.

§. 3. [*To the great terror and disturbance of the Kings leige people and Subjects, and the evil example of all others in the like case offending, against the Kings peace, his Crown, and Dignity.*]

Were these black Criminations as true as they are wretchedly false, we should give as just an occasion, to loose our Liberties, as our cruel Adversaries are ready to take any to deprive us unjustly of them. O ! How notorious is it to all sober people, that our manner of life is far from terrifying any ; and how absurd to think that naked men (in the generality of their conversation, known to be harmless and quiet) should prove a terror or disturbance to the People ; certainly, if any such thing should be in the time of our Meetings, it is brought with the cruelty and barbarous actions of your own Souldiers ; they never learned by our example to beat, hale before Magistrates, fine, and imprison for matters relating to Gods Worship; neither can they say, we are their Presidents; for all those *Adulterous, Prodigal, Lascivious, Drunken, Swearing,* and *Prophane acts they daily commit, and esteem rather occasion of brag and boast, then sorrow and repentance*: No, they need not go so far, they have too many (God Almighty knows) of their own Superiors for their example.

§. 4. But we can never pass over with silence, nor enough observe the detestable juggle of such Indictments, which we require all *English and Conscientious men* to mind as they value themselves in the like occasion. How little a grain of fact was proved, yet how spatious an Indictment was made? had it related to the evidence, the bulk had been excusable; but when it only swelled with malicious scaring Phrases, to suggest to the people, that they were the meerest Villains, the most dangerous Persons, and designing mutually the subversion of the Laws, and breach of the Peace, to the terrifying of the People, &c.

Who can choose but tell them of their Romance-Indictment, that is so forged, as it truly merits another against itself. This they childishly call *Form*; but had an *Italian*, or other Stranger been in Court, he would have judged it matter of fact, as thinking it unworthy of a Kings Court, to accuse men in terms, not legally, truly, or probably due to the fact they really had committed; as well as that no Court would practise it, but that which loved to deprive men of their Liberties and Lives, rather then to save them; *Nolens Volens.*

§. 5. Had their cruelty and juggle ended here itself, they would have spared us the pain of any further observation. But that which we have to add, on the Prisoners behalf, renders their actions so abominable, in the sight of Justice, that all honest and ingenious hearts must needs abhor their base Snares.

5

They tell the Jury, *That being but Judges of fact only, they were to bring the Prisoners in guilty* (that is of the fact) *at their peril ; and it was the part of the Bench, to judge what was Law* : So that if the Jury had brought them in *Guilty*, without any further additional explanation (though intentionally they meant only of the fact proved by evidence) yet the Bench would have extended it to every part of the Indictment, and by this impious delusion, to have perjured a well meaning Jury, and have had their barbarous ends upon the innocent Prisoners. But the Jury better understanding themselves brought in *Will. Penn* guilty of the fact proved, namely, *That he was speaking to some people met in* Gratious-Church-Street, *but not of an unlawful Assembly, so circumstantiated* (the mention of which stabbed their design of moulding the general answer of *guilty* to their own ends, to the heart) nor indeed could they do otherwise ; for as well the Jury as Prisoners, were denied to have any Law produced, by which, they might measure the Truth of the Indictment, and guilt of the fact. But because the Recorder would or could not (perhaps tis so long since he read Law, that he may have forgotten it) we shall perform his part, in shewing what is that *Common Law of the Land*, which in general, he said, they were Indicted for the breach of, and which indeed, if rightly understood, is the undoubted Birth-right of every English-man ; yea, the Inheritance of Inheritances, *Major Hæreditas venit unicuiq ; nostrum a Jure et Legibus, quam a Parentibus.* Cook, *Inst.* 2. 56.

§. 6. All the various kinds or models of Government, that are in the World, stand either upon *Will* and *Power*, or *Condition* and *Contract*, the first, rule by men, the second, by Laws : It is our happiness to be born under such a constitution, as is most abhorrent in it self, of all arbitrary Government, and which is, and ever has been, most choice and careful of her Laws, by which all Right is preserved.

§. 7. All Laws are either Fundamental, and so immut-able, or Superficial, and so alterable. By the first we understand such Laws, as injoyn men to be just, honest, ver-tuous ; to do no wrong, to kill, rob, deceive, prejudice none ; but to do, as one would be done unto ; to cherish good, and to terrifie wicked men ; in ·short, universal Reason, *which are not subject to any revolutions, because no emergency, time, or occasion can ever justifie a suspention of their execution, much less their utter Abrogation.*

§. 8. By Superficial Laws we understand, such Acts, Laws, or Statutes, as are suited to present occurrances ; and which may as well be abrogated, for the good of the King-dom, as they were first made for it. For instance, those Statutes, that relate to Victuals, Cloaths, and places of Trade, &c. which have ever stood whilst the reason of them was in force, but when that benefit, which once redounded, fell by cross occurrances, they ended according to that old Maxim, *Cessante ratione Legis, cessat Lex ;* but this cannot be said of Fundamental Laws, *Till Houses stand without their Foundations, and English man-kind wholly cease to be,* which brings close upon the point.

§. 9. There is not any Country, that has more con-stantly exprest her care and deep solicitude, to the preserva-vation of her fundamental Laws, then the *English* Nation ; and though the evil of some particular times and persons have endeavoured an utter Abolition of those excellent Fundamentals, which we have before defined and defended from any just reason of revolution ; yet God Almighty, who is alwayes concerned to avenge the cause of Justice, and those excellent good Laws, by which it is upheld, has by his providence befool'd their contrivances, & baffled their attempts, by bringing their designs to naught, and their persons frequently to condign punishment and disgrace,

their Age no Antiquary living can assure, us unless they say,
As old as Reason it self; but our own Authors are not
lacking to inform us, that the Liberties, Properties and
Priviledges of the *English* Nation are very ancient.

§. 10. For *Horn* in his *Mirror of Justice* (writ in *Edward*
the first's time) *Fol.* 1. tells us, " That after God had abated
" the Nobility of the *Britans*, he did deliver the Realm to
" men more humble and simple, of the Countries adjoyning,
" to wit, the *Saxons*, which came from the parts of *Almaign*
" to conquer this Land, of which men there were forty Sove-
" raigns which did rule as Companions; and those Princes
" did call this Realm *England*, which before was named the
" Greater *Britan*: These after great wars, tribulations and
" pains, by long time suffered, did choose a King to raign
" over them, to govern the people of God, and to maintain
" and defend their persons, and their good in quiet, by the
" Rules of Right; and at the beginning they did cause him
" to sware to maintain the holy Christian Faith, and to guide
" his people by Right, with all his power, without respect of
" persons, and to observe the Laws: And after when the
" Kingdom was turned into an Heritage; King *Alfred*, that
" governed this Kingdom about an hundred seventy one
" years before the Conquest, did cause the great men of the
" Kingdom to assemble at *London*, and there did ordain for a
" perpetual usage, That twice in the Year, or oftner, if need
" should be, in time of Peace, they should assemble at *London*
" in Parliament; for the Government of Gods People, that
" men might live in quiet, and receive right by certain
" usages, and holy Judgments.

" In which Parliament (saith our Author) the Rights and
" Prerogatives of the Kings and of the Subjects are dis-
" tinguished and set apart; and particularly by him ex-
" pressed, too tedious here to insert; amongst which
" Ordinances we find, " That no man should be imprisoned,

" but for a capital Offence. And if a man should detain
" another in Prison, by colour of right (where there was none)
" till the party imprisoned died ; he that kept him in Prison
" should be held guilty of murder, as you may read pag. 33.
And pag. 36. " He is declared guilty of Homicide, by
" whom a man shall die in prison, whether it be the Judges,
" that shall too long delay to do a man right, or by cruelty of
" Goalers, or suffering him to die of Famine ; or when a man
" is adjudged to do pennance, and shall be surcharged by his
" Goaler with Irons, or other pain, whereof he is deprived of
" his life. And p. 149. That by the antient Law of *Eng-*
" *land,* it was Fellony to detain a man in prison, after suffi-
" cient Bale offered ; where the party was plevisable ; every
" person was plevisable, but he that was appealed of Treason,
" Murder, Robbery or Burglary, pag. 35. None ought to
" be put in common Prisons, but only such as were AT-
" TAINTED, or principally APPEALED or INDICTED
" of some capital Offence, or ATTAINTED of false or
" wrongfull Imprisonment ; so tender have the ancient
" Laws and Constitutions of this Realm been of the Liberty
" of their Subjects persons, that no man ought to be Im-
" prisoned, but for a Capital Offence, as, *Treason, Murder,*
" *Robbery,* or *Burglary.*

§. 11. Nor is *Lambard* short in his excellent translation
of the Saxon Laws, from *King Ina's* time, 712. to *Hen.* 3.
1100. In describing to us the great Obligation, and strong
Condition, the people were wont to put upon their Kings,
To observe the ancient fundamental Laws, and free Customs of
this Land, which were handed down from one Age to another.
And in the 17th Chap. of *Edw.* the Confessors Laws, the mention there made of a Kings duty is very remarkable. That if
he break his Oath, or performed not his Obligation (*Nec*
nomen Regis in eo constabit) The same *Lambard* further tells

us, that however any may affirm *William* of *Normandy* to be a Conqueror ; *He was received by the people as* Edwards *Successor, and by solemn Oath taken, to maintain unto them the same Laws that his Kinsman* Edward *the Confessor did ;* this doctrine remained in the general, unquestioned, to the reign of *King John*, who imperiously thought that *Voluntas Regis* and not *Salvus Populi*, was *Suprema Lex*, or the Kings will was the supream Law, and not the Peoples Preservation; till the incensed Barons of that time, betook themselves to a vigorous defence of their antient Rights and Liberties, and learnt him to keep those Laws by a due restraint and timely compulsion, which his former invasion of them evidenced to the World he would never have done willingly.

§. 12. The Proposals and Articles of agreement, with the Pledges given to the Barons, on the behalf of the People by the King, were confirm'd in *Hen.* the 3ds. time, his Son and Successor ; *When the abused, slighted, and disregarded Laws by his Father*, were thought fit to be reduced to record, *that the people of* England *might not forever after be to seek for a written recorded Law, to their defence and security* ; for, *Misera servitus est ubi jus est vagum aut incognitum* ; and so we enter upon that *grand Charter of Liberty and Priviledge*, in the Cause, Reason, and End of it.

§. 1. We shall first rehearse it, so far as we are concerned (with the formalities of *Grant* and *Curse*) and shall then say something as to the Cause, Reason and End of it.

A Rehersal of the Material Parts of the Great Charter of *England*.

HEnry, *by the Grace of God, King of* England &c. *To all Arch-bishops, or Earls, Barons, Sheriffs, Provosts, Officers, and to all Bailiffs, and our faithfull Subjects who shall see this present Charter, greeting.* Know ye that we unto the honour of Almighty God, and for the Salvation of the Souls of our Progenitors, and our Successors, Kings of *England*, to the advancement of holy Church, and amendment of our Realm, of our meer and free will have given and granted *to all Arch-Bishops, &c. and to all Free-men of this our Realm*, these Liberties, under-written, to be holden and kept in this our Realm of *England* for evermore.

We have granted and given to all Free-men of our Realm for us and our Heirs for evermore, these Liberties under-written to have and to hold to them, and to their Heirs, of us and our Heirs fore-nam'd.

A Free-man shall not be Amerced for a smal fault, *but after the quantity of the fault.* And for a great fault, *after the manner thereof*, saving to him his Contenements or Free-hold. And a Merchant likewise shall be amerced, *saving to him his Merchandize*, and none of the said Amercements shall be assessed, *but by the Oath of good and honest men of the Vicinage.*

No Free-man shall be taken, or imprisoned, nor be disseized of his Free-hold, or Liberties, or free Customs or be Outlawed, or Exiled, or any other wayes destroyed; nor we shall not pass upon him, nor condemn him, *but by lawful judgment of his Peers*, or by the Law of the Land ; *we shall sell to no man, we shall deny nor defer to no man either Justice or Right.*

9 H. 3.
Confirm'd
28 Ed. 3.

Chap. 1.
the form
of anc-
ient Acts,
&c. Co.
2 Inst.,
fol. 2.
Chap. 14.

Cha. 29.

And to all these Customs, Liberties aforesaid, which we have granted to be holden within this our Realm, as much as appertaineth to us and our Heirs we shall observe ; and all men of this our Realm, as well Spiritual as Temporal, (as much as in them is) shall observe the same against all persons in likewise. And for this our Gift, and Grant of these Liberties, and for other contained in our Charter of Liberties of our *Forrest*, the Arch-Bishops, Bishops, Abots, Priors, Earls, Barons, Knights, Free-holders, and other our Subjects, have given unto us the fifteenth part of all their moveables ; *And we have granted unto them on the other part, that neither we, nor our Heirs, shall procure or do anything whereby the Liberties in this Charter contained shall be infringed or broken* ; and if any thing be procured by any person contrary to the Premises, *shall be had of no force nor effect* These being Witnesses, *Boniface* Arch-Bishop of *Canterbury*, &c. We ratifying and approving those Gifts and Grants aforesaid, confirm and make strong all the same, *for us and our Heirs perpetually*, and by the Tenor of these Presents do renew the same willingly ; and granting for us and our Heirs, that this Charter, in all and singular his Articles for evermore shall be stedfastly, firmly, and inviolably observed, *And if any Article in the same Charter contained, yet hitherto peradventure hath not been observed, nor kept, we will, and by our Authority Royal command from henceforth firmly, they be observed.* Witness, &c.

The Sentence of Curse given by the Bishops, with the Kings consent, against the Breakers of the great Charter.

I *N the year of our Lord* 1253. *the third day of May, in the great Hall of the King at* Westminster, *in the presence, and by the consent of the Lord* Henry, *by the grace of God, King of* England, *and the Lord* Richard, *Earl of* Cornwall, *his Brother ;* Roger Bigot, *Earl of* Norfolk *Marshal of* England ; Humphry, *Earl of* Hereford ; Henry, *Earl of* Oxford ; John, *Earl Warren* ; *and other Estates of the Realm of* England : *We* Boniface, *by the mercy of God, Arch-Bishop* of Canterbury, *Primate of* England, F. *of* London, H. *of* Ely, S. *of* Worcester, E. *of* Lincoln, W. *of* Norwich, P. *of* Hereford, W. *of* Salesbury, W. *of Durham,* R. *of* Excester, M. *of* Carlile, W. *of* Bath, E. *of* Rochester, T. *of St.* Davids, *Bishops. apparelled in Pontificals, with Tapers burning, against the Breakers of the Churches Liberties, and of the Liberties and other Customs of this Realm of* England ; *and namely these which are contained in the Charter of the common Liberties of* England, *and Charter of the* Forrest, *have denounced Sentence of Excommunication in this form, by the Authority of Almighty God, the Father, the Son, and the Holy Ghost, &c. of the blessed Apostles* Peter *and* Paul, *and of all Apostles, and of all Martyrs, of blessed* Edw. *King of* England, *and of all the Saints of Heaven, We Excommunicate and Accurse, and from the benefits of our holy Mother the Church we sequester all those that hereafter willingly and maliciously deprive or spoil the Church of her Right ; and all those that by any craft, or willingness, do violate, break, dimin-*

ish, or change the Churches Liberties, and free Customs contained in the Charters of the common Liberties, and of the Forrest, granted by our Lord the King, to Arch-Bishops, Bishops, and other Prelates of England, and likewise to the Earls, Barons, Knights, and other Free-holders of the Realm ; and all that secretly and openly, by deed, word or counsel do make Statutes, or observe them being made, and that bring in Customs to keep them, when they be brought in, against the said Liberties, or any of them, and all those that shall presume to judge against them ; and all and every such person before mentioned, that wittingly shall commit any thing of the premises, let them well know that they incur the aforesaid Sentence ipso facto.

A Confirmation of the Charters and Liberties of *England,* and of the *Forrest,* made the twenty fifth year of *Edward* the first.

E *Dward,* by the Grace of God, King of *England,* Lord of *Ireland,* Duke of *Guyan,* To all those that these present Letters shall hear or see, greeting, Know ye that we to the honour of God, and to the profit of our Realm, have granted for us, and our Heirs, and the Charter of Liberties, and the Charter of the Forrest, which were made by common assent of all the Realm, in the time of King *Henry* our Father, shall be kept in every point, without breach ; and we will that the same Charters shall be sent under our Seal, as well to our Justices of the Forrest, as to others, and to all Sheriffs of Shires, and to all our other Officers, and to all our Cities throughout the Realm, together with our Writs, in the which it shall be contained, that they cause the aforesaid Charters to be published, and to declare to the People, that we have confirmed them in all points ; and that our Justices, Sheriffs, Mayors, and other Ministers, which under us have the Laws of our Land to guide, shall allow the same Charters pleaded before them in Judgment, in all their points ; that is, to wit, the great Charter, as the Common Law, and the Charter of our Forrest, for the *Welch* of our Realm.

And we will, that if any judgment be given from henceforth, contrary to the points of the Charter aforesaid, by the Justices, or by any other of our Ministers, that hold Plea before them, against the points of the Charters, it shall be undone, and holden for naught.

And we will that the same Charters shall be sent under our Seal to Cathedral Churches throughout our Realm, there to remain, and shall be read before the people two times by the year.

And that all Arch-bishops and Bishops shall pronounce the Sentence of Excommunication against all those that by word, deed or counsel do contrary to the foresaid Charters, or that in any point do break or undo them ; And that the said Curses be twice a year denounced and published by the Prelates aforesaid ; and if the same Prelates or any of them be remiss in the denunciation of the said Sentences, the Arch-bishops of *Canterbury* and *York*, for the time being, shall compel and distrain them to the execution of their duties in form aforesaid.

The Sentence of the Clergy against the Breakers of the Articles above-mentioned.

IN the Name of the Father, the Son, and the Holy Ghost, Amen : Whereas our Soveraign Lord the King, to the honour of God, and of holy Church, and for the common profit of the Realm, hath granted for him, and his Heirs for ever, these Articles above-written : Robert *Arch-Bishop of* Canterbury, *Primate of all* England, *admonished all his Province once twice and thrice, because that shortness will not suffer so much delay, as to give knowledge to all the People of* England, *of these presents in writing : we therefore enjoyn all Persons, of what estate soever that be, that they, and every of them, as much as in them is, shall uphold and maintain these Articles granted by our Soveraign Lord the King, in all points : And all those that in any point do resist, or break, or in any manner hereafter Procure, Counsel, or in any wise Assent to Testifie or Break those Ordinances, or go about it, by word or deed, openly or privily, by any manner of pretence or colour ; we, the aforesaid Arch-Bishop, by our Authority in this Writing expressed, do Excommunicate and Accurse, and from the Body of our Lord Jesus Christ, and from all the Company of Heaven, and from all the Sacraments of Holy Church do sequester and exclude.*

We may here see, that in the obscurest Times of sottish Popery, they were not left without a sence of Justice, and the necessity of *Liberty* and *Property*, to be inviolably enjoy'd which brings us to the cause of it.

1st   The cause of this famous Charter, was, as we have already said, the Incroachments that were made by several

Ministers of precedent Kings, that almost became Customary and which had neer extinguisht the free Customs due to Englishmen : How great care it cost our Ancestors, it unbecomes us to ignore, or by our silence to neglect ; It was the *Yoak* and *Muzzle*, which failed not to dis-able many rageing Bears, from entring *the pleasant Vineyard of English Freedoms*, that otherwise would not have left a fruitful Vine in being. Anon we may give the Reader an account of some, with their Wages as well as Works.

2d The Reason of it, is so great, that it seems to be its own. It is the very *Image* and *Expression of Justice, Liberty,* and *Property* ; Points of such eminent importance, as without which no Government can be said to be Reasonable, but arbitrary, and tyrannical. It allows every man that Liberty God and Nature hav given him, and the secure possession of his property, from the In-road or Invasion of his Neighbour, or any else of that constitution. It justifies no man in a fault, only it provides equal and just wayes to have the Offender tryed ; considering the malice of many Prosecutors, and the great value of Liberty and Life.

3d The End of it was the most noble of any earthly projection, to wit, *The refixing of those shaken Laws*, held for many hundred years, by constant claim, that they living might be re-enstated in their primitive liberty, and their posterity secured in the possession of so great a happiness.

Amongst those many rich Advantages, that accrew to the free People of *England*, from this Great Charter ; and those many confirmatory Statutes of the same, we shall present the Reader with the sight of some few, that may most properly fall, under the consideration and inquiry of these present times, as found in our Common Law Books.

1st [*That every English-man is born free.*]

2d [*That no such Free-man shall be taken, attached, assessed, or imprisoned, by any Petition or Suggestion to the King or his Counsel, unless by the indictment or presentment of good and lawful men, where such deeds be done*] 5 Edw. 3. Chap. 9. 25 Edw. 3. Chap. 4. 17 R. 2. Chap. 6. Rot. Parl. 42 Edw. 3. *Cook, 2. Inst.* 46.

3d [*That no Free-man shall be disseized of his Free-hold, or Liberties, or free Customs, &c.* hereby is intended, saith *Cook,* That *Lands, Tenements, Goods, and Chattels.*] shall not be seised into the Kings hands contrary to this Great Charter, &c. 43. Ass. page 12. 43 *Edward* 3. *Cook, 2 Inst.* 32. Neither shall any such Free-man be put from his Livelyhood without answer, *Cook, 2 Inst.* 47.

4ly [*That no Free-man shall be out-lawed.*] *unless he shroud and hide himself voluntarily from the justice of the Law,* 2 & 3 Phil. & Mar. Dier. 114. 145.

5ly [*No Free-man shall be exiled.*] Cook says there are but two Grounds, upon which any man may be exiled : One by Act of Parliament (supposing it not contrary to the great Charter.)——the other in case of abjuration, for Fellony by the Common Law, &c. *Cook, 2 Inst.* 47.

6ly [*No Free-man shall be destroyed,* that is, he shall not be *fore-judged of Life, Limb, Dis-herited, or put to Torture, or Death*] every oppression against Law, by colour of any usurped Authority, is a kind of Destruction, and it is the worst oppression that is done by colour of Justice. *Cook Instit.* 2. 48.

7ly [*That no Free-man shall be thus taken, or imprisoned, dis eized, out-lawed, exiled, or destroyed of his Liberties, Free-holds, and free Customs, but BY THE LAWFULL JUDG-MENT OF HIS PEERS*] (vulgarly called *Jury.*) So that the Judgment of any fact or person, is by this fundamental

Law, referred to the Brests and Consciences of the Jury; Its rendred in Latine *PER LEGALE JVDICIVM*, that is, *Lawful Judgment*; from whence it is to be observed, that the Judgment must have Law in it, and be according to Law, which cannot be where they are not Judges, how far the fact is Legal or the contrary; *Judicium quasi Juris Dictum* [*The Voice of Law and Right*] And therefore is their Verdict not to be rejected, because it is supposed to be the Truth, according to their Consciences: For *Verdict* is from *vere dictum,* is *quasi dictum veritatis,* [or *a true saying or Judgment*] 9 *Hen.* 3. 29. *Cook Inst.* 1. 32. *Inst.* 4. 207. *Cook* says, that by the word LEGALE three things are implyed.

(1st) *That this was by Law, before the Statute, and therefore this Statute but declaratory of the antient Law.*

(2d) That their Verdict must be legally given ; wherein is to be observed. (1st) *The Jury ought to hear no Evidence, but in the hearing and presence of the Prisoner.* (2d) *That they cannot send to ask any Question in Law of the Judges, but in the presence of the Prisoner ; for, de facto Jus oritur*

(3d) The Evidence produced by the Kings Counsel, being given, *the Judges cannot collect the Evidence, nor urge it by way of charge to the Jury, nor yet confer with the Jury about the Evidence, but in the presence of the Prisoner,* Cook. Inst. 2. 49.

8th [*Or by the Law of the Land*] It is a *Synonimous* expression, importing no more *then by a Tryal of Peers or a Jury*; for it is sometimes rendred not (*or*) disjunctively, but (*and*) which is connectively ; however, it can never signifie any thing contrary to the old way of trying by Peers ; for then it would be connected to a contradiction.

Besides, *Cook* well observes, that in the 4th Chap. of the 25th *Edw.* 3. *Per Legem Terræ,* imports no more then a Tryal by due process, and writ Original at Common Law, which cannot be without a *Jury*; therefore, *Per Judicium parum & per Legem Terræ*, signifies the same priviledge unto the people, *Cook Inst.* 2. pag. 50.

Thus have we presented you with some of those maxims of Law, dearer to our Ancestors then life, *Because they are the defence of the Lives and Liberties of the People of* England; it is from this 29th Chap. of the Great Charter; *Great,* not for its Bulk, but the Priviledges in it; as from a spatious Root, that so many fruitful Branches of the Law of *England* springs, if *Cook* may be credited. But how *sacred* soever they have been esteemed, and still are by noble and just minds, yet so degenerate are some, in their proceedings, that conscious to themselves of their baseness, they will not dare stand the touch of this great Charter, and those just Laws grounded upon it, of which number we may truly rank the Mayor and Recorder of *London*, with the rest of their wise Companions, in this late Sessions at the *Old-Baily*, upon the occasion of the Prisoners.

First, The Prisoners were taken, and imprisoned without Presentment of good and Lawfull men of the Vicinage, or the Neighbourhood, *but after a military and tumultuous manner, contrary to the Grand Charter.*

2d *They refused to produce the* Law *upon which they proceeded,* leaving thereby the Prisoners, *Jury,* and the whole Assembly in the dark.

3d *They refused the Prisoners to plead,* and directly withstood that great Priviledge, mentioned in the first Chap. 25 *Edw.* 1. *Where all Justices, Mayors, Sheriffs, and other Ministers that have the Laws of the Land to guide them, are required to allow the said Charter to be pleaded in all its points, and in all causes that shall come before them in Judgment.* For no sooner did *William Penn,* or his Fellow Prisoner, urge upon them the great Charter, and other good Laws, but the

8

Recorder cryed, Take him away, take him away, put him into the Bale-dock or Hole ; from which the Recorder can never deliver himself, unless it be by avowing ; *the Laws are not his Guide, and therefore does not suffer them to be pleaded before him in Judgment.*

4ly *They gave the Jury their charge, in the Prisoners absence, endeavouring highly to insence the Jury against them.*

5ly The verdict being given, which is in Law, DICTUM VERITATIS (*The voice of Truth her self*) (because not sutable to their humor) *They did five times reject it, with many abusive imperious, and menacing Expressions to the Jury,* (such as no president can afford us) as if they were not the only constituted Judges by the Fundamental Laws of the Land, *but meer Cyphers only to signifie something behind their Figures.*

6ly Though the Prisoners were cleared by their Jury, yet were they continued for the non-payment of their Fines, laid upon them, for not pulling off their Hats, in which the Law is notoriously broken.

(1st) *In that no man shall be amerced, but according to the Offence ; and they have fined each forty Marks.*

(2d) *They were not merced by any Jury, but at the will of an incensed Bench.*

Besides there is no Law against the Hat, and where there is no Law there can be no Transgression, and consequently no legal Amercement or Fine. 9 *Hen.* 3. chap. 14. But how the Prisoners were trapanned into it, is most ridiculous on the side of the contrivers, that finding their Hats off, would have them put on again by their Officers, to fool the Prisoners, with a trial of putting them off again ; which Childish conceit not being gratified, they fined them the forty Marks a piece.

7ly   Instead of accepting their Verdict as good in Law, and for the true decission of the matter, according to the great Charter (that constitutes them proper Judges, and which bears them out, with many other good Laws, in what they agreed to, as a Verdict) the Court did most illegally, and tyrannically fine and imprison them, as in the Tryal was exprest.   And that notwithstanding the late just resentment of the House of Commons, in Judge *Keelings* Case, where they resolved, that the president and practise of Fining and Imprisoning of *Juries, for their Verdicts, were illegal.*   And here we must needs observe two things.

(1st)   That the Fundamental Laws of *England* cannot be more slighted, and contradicted in any thing (next Englishmen being quite destroyed) then in not suffering them to have that equal *medium*, or just way of tryal, that the same Law has provided, *which is by a Jury.*

(2d)   That the late proceedings of the Court, at the Old-Baily, is an evident Demonstration, that Juries are now but *meer Formality*, and that the partial Charge of the Bench must be the Verdict of the Jury ; *for if ever a Rape were attempted on the Consciences of any Jury, it was there.*   And indeed the ignorance of Jurors of their Authority by Law, is the only Reason of their unhappy cringing to the Court, and being scared into an *Anti-Conscience Verdict*, by their lawless threats.

But we have lived to an Age, so deboist from all humanity and reason, as well as Faith and Religion, that some stick not to turn *Butchers to their Priviledges, and Conspirators against their own Liberties.*   For however *Magna Charta* had once the Reputation of a sacred unalterable Law, and few hardned enough, to incur and bear the long Curse, that attends the Violaters of it, yet it is frequently objected now, that the benefits, there designed *are but temporary*, and therefore lyable to alteration as other Statues are. *What Game such persons play at, may be lively read, in the attempts of* Dyonifius, Phalaris, &c. *which would have Will and Power be the peoples Law.*

But that the Priviledges due to *English*-men, by the great Charter of *England*, have their Foundation in Reason and Law ; and that those new *Cassandrian* wayes, to introduce *Will* and *Power* deserve to be detested by all persons professing sence and honesty, and the least Allegiance to our *English* Government ; we shall make appear from a sober consideration of the nature of those Priviledges contained in that *Charter*.

(1) The Ground of alteration of any Law in Government (where there is no invasion) should arise from the universal *discommodity of its continuance*, but there can be no disprofit in the discontinuance of *Liberty* and *Property*, *therefore there can be no just ground of alteration.*

(2) No one *English*-man is born Slave to another, neither has the one a right to inherit the sweat and benefit of the others labour (without consent) *therefore the Liberty and Property of an* English-*man cannot reasonably be at the will and beck of another, let his quality and rank be never so great.*

(3) *There can be nothing more unreasonable then that which is partial*, but to take away the LIBERTY and PROPERTY of any (which are natural Rights) without breaking the Law of *Nature* (and not of Will and Power) is manifestly partial, *and therefore unreasonable.*

(4) If it be just and reasonable *for men to do as they would be done by*, then no sort of men should invade the Liberties and Properties of other men, because they would not be served so themselves.

(5) Where Liberty and Property are destroyed there must alwayes be a state of Force and War, which however pleasing it may be unto the *Invaders*, it will be esteemed intolerable by the *Invaded*, who will no longer remain subject in all humane probability, then while they want as much power to free themselves, as their Adversaries had to enslave them : *The troubles, hazards, ill-consequences, and illegality of such attempts as they have declined by the most prudent in all Ages, so have they proved most easie to the most savage of all Nations, who first or last have by a mighty Torent freed themselves, to the due punishment and great infamy of their Oppressors* ; such being the advantage, such the disadvantage which necessarily do attend the fixation, and removal of Liberty and Property.

We shall proceed to make it appear that *Magna Charta* (as recited by us) imports nothing less than their preservation.

No Free-men shall be taken, or imprisoned or be disseized of his Freehold, or Liberties, or free Customs, or be out-lawed, or exiled, or any other wayes destroyed ; nor we will not pass upon him, nor condemn him, but by lawful judgment of his Peers, &c.

A Free-man shall be amerced for a small fault, but after the manner of the fault ; and for a great fault, after the greatness thereof, and none of the said amercement shall be assessed, but by the Oath of good and lawfull men of the Vicinage.

First, It asserts *English*-men to be free ; *that's Liberty.*

Secondly, That they have Free-holds, *that's Property.*

Thirdly, That Amercement, or Penalties should be proportioned to the faults committed, *which is Equity.*

Fourthly, That they shall lose neither, but when they are adjudged to have forfeited them, in the judgment of their honest Neighbours, according to the Law of the Land ; *which is lawfull Judgment.*

It is easie to discern to what pass the Enemies of the *great Charter* would bring the People of *England.*

First, They are now Free-men ; *but they would have them Slaves.*

Secondly, They have now right unto their *Wives, Children,* and *Estates,* as their undoubted property ; *but such would rob and spoil them of all.*

Thirdly, Now no man is to be amerced, or punished, but suitable to his fault ; *whilst they would make it suitable to their revengeful minds, and unlimitted wills.*

Fourthly, Whereas the Power of Judgment lies in the Brests and Consciences of twelve honest Neighbours ; *they would have it at the discretion of mercenary Judges :* To which, we cannot chuse but add, *That such Discourses manifestly strike at this present constitution of Government* ; for it being founded upon the *Great Charter* (which is the Antient Common Law of the Land) as upon its best Foundation ; none can design the cancelling of the *Charter,* but they must necessarily intend the extirpation of the *English Government :* For where the cause is taken away the effect must consequently cease. *And as the restauration of our antient English Laws, by the* Great Charter, *was the soveraign Balsom which cured our former breaches, so doubtless will the continuation of it prove an excellent prevention to any future disturbances.*

But some are ready to object, *That the Great Charter consisting as well of Religious as civil Rights, the former having received an alteration, there is the same reason, why the latter may have the like.*

To which we answer, That the reason of alteration cannot be the same, therefore the consequence is false. The one being matter of Opinion, about Faith and Religious Worship, which is as various, as the unconstant apprehensions of men; but the other is matter of so immutable right, and justice, that all Generations (however differing in their religious Opinion) have concentered and agreed to the *certainty, equity,* and *indispensable necessity of preserving these fundamental Laws;* so that *Magna Charta* hath risen and fallen with the differing religious Opinions that have been in this Land, but have ever remained, *as the stable right of every individual English-man, purely as an English-man.* Otherwise, If the civil *Priviledges* of the People, had fallen with the pretended Religious Priviledges of the *Popish Tyranny,* at the first Reformation (as must needs be suggested by this Objection) our case had ended here, *that we had obtained a Spiritual Freedom, at the cost of a Civil bondage;* which certainly was far from the intention of the first Reformers, and probably an unseen consequence, by the Objectors to their idle Opinion.

In short, There is no time, in which any man may plead the necessity of such an Action, as is unjust in its own nature, which he must unavoidably be guilty of, *That doth deface or cancel that Law by which the justice of Liberty and Property is confirmed and maintained to the People.* And consequently, no person may legally attempt the subversion, or extenuation of the force of the *Great Charter.* We shall proceed to prove from instances out of both.

1st *Any Judgment given contrary to the said Charter, is to be undone, and holden for nought.* 25 Edw. 1 *Chap.* 2.

2d *Any that by Word, Deed, or Counsel, go contrary to the said* Charter, *are to be excommunicated by the Bishops: And* the *Arch-Bishops of* Canterbury *and* York, *are bound to compel the other Bishops to denounce Sentence accordingly, in case of their remissness, or neglect ;* which certainly hath relation to the State rather then the Church ; *since there was never any necessity of compelling the Bishops to denounce Sentence in their own case, though frequently in the peoples,* 25 Edw. 1. *Chap.* 4.

3d *That the great* Charter, *and* Charter *of Forrest, be holden and kept in all Points, and if any Statute be made to the contrary, that it shall be holden for nought.* 43 Edw. 3. 1. Upon which *Cook,* that famous English Lawyer, said, *That albeit Judgments in the Kings Courts, are of high regard in Law, and* Judicia *are accounted as* Juris Dicta ; *yet it is provided by Act of Parliament, That if any Judgment be given contrary to any of the points of the great Charter, it shall be holden for nought.*

He further saith, *That upon the Statute of the 25th* Edw. 1. *Chapter* 1. *That this great* Charter, *and the* Charter *of Forrest, are properly the Common Law of this Land, or the Law is Common to all the People thereof.*

4ly Another Statute runs thus, *If any Force come to disturb the execution of the Common Law, ye shall cause their bodies to be arrested, and put in Prison ; Ye shall deny no man right by the Kings Letters, nor counsel the King any thing that may turn to his damage or disherison.* 18 Edw. 3. *Chap.* 7. *Neither to delay Right by any command under the great or little Seal.* This is the Judges Charge and Oath. 2 *Edw.* 3. chap. 8. 14 *Ed.* 3. 14. 11 *R.* 2. chap. 10.

5ly Such care hath been taken, for the preservation of this great Charter, that in the 25th of *Edw.* 1. It was enacted, *That Commissioners should issue forth, that there should be chosen in every Shire-Court, by the commonalty of the same Shire, three substantial men, Knights, or other lawful, wise, and well disposed persons, to be Justices, which shall be assigned by the Kings Letters, Patents, under the great Seal, to hear and determine (without any other Writ, but only their Commission) such plaints as shall be made upon all those, that commit, or offend against any point, contained in the aforesaid* Charters, 21 Edw. 1. chap. 1.

6ly   The necessity of preserving these *Charters*, hath appeared in nothing more, than in the care they have taken to confirm them ; which as *Cook* observes, hath been by thirty two *Parliaments Confirmed, Established, and Commanded to be put in execution*, with the condign punishment they had inflicted upon the Offenders.   *Cooks Proem*, to the second Book of his Inst.

7ly   That in the notable *Petition of Right*, many of these great Priviledges, and free Customs, contained in the aforesaid Charters, and other good Laws, *are recited and confirmed*, 3 Car. 1.

8ly   The late King, in his Declaration, at *New-Market*, 1641, acknowledged *the Law to be the Rule of his Power*.   By which he doubtless intended *Fundamental Laws*, since it may be the great advantage of Countries, sometimes to suspend the execution of *temporary Laws*.

Having so manifestly evidenced that *venerable esteem*, our Ancestors had of that *Golden Rule* (the Great Charter) with their deep solicitude, to preserve it from the defacing of Usurpation and Faction.   We shall proceed to give an account of their just resentment and earnest prosecution against some of those, who in any Age have adventured, to undermine that antient Foundation, by introducing an arbitrary way of Government.

1st   As Juditious *Lambard* reports in his *Saxon* Translation ; *That the Kings in those dayes, were by their Coronation-*

Oaths obliged to keep the Antient Fundamental Laws and Customs of this Land (of which this great Charter is but declaratory) so *did* King Alfred (reputed the most famous Compiler of Laws amongst them) *give this discovery of his indignation against his own Judges, for actions contrary to those Fundamental Laws, that he commanded the execution of forty of them;* which may be a seasonable *Caveat* to the Judges of our times.

2d *Hubert de Burgo,* once chief Justice of *England* (having advised *Edw.* I. in the eleventh year of his reign, (in his Counsel holden at *Oxford, To cancel this great Charter, and that of the Forrest*) was *justly sentenced according to Law, by his Peers, in open Parliament.* When the Statute called CONFIRMATIONIS CARTARUM was made, in the first Chapter whereof, *Magna Charta,* is peculiarly called, the *Common Law.* 25 *Edw,* I. Chap. 2.

3d The *Spencers,* (both Father and Son) for their arbitrary domination, and rash, and evil counsel to *Edw.* the 2d (by which he was seduced to break the great *Charter*) were banished for their pains, as Cook relates.

4ly The same fate attended *Tresillian* and *Belknap,* for their illegal proceedings.

5ly The Breach of this great Charter, was the ground of that exemplary Justice, done upon *Empson* and *Dudley,* whose case is very memorable in this point ; *For though they gratified* Hen. 7. *in what they did, and had an Act of Parliament for their Warrant, made the eleventh of his reign; yet met they with their due reward from the hands of Justice, that Act being against Equity and common Reason, and so no justifiable Ground or Apology, for those frequent Abuses, and Opressions of the People, they were found guilty of.* Hear what the Lord *Cook* further saith, concerning the matter

" There was an Act of Parliament, made in the eleventh year
" of King *Hen* 7. which had a *fair flattering Preamble*, pre-
" tending to avoid divers mischiefs, which were (1st) *The*
" *high displeasure of Almighty God* (2d) *The great Let of the*
" *Common Law*, And (3d) *The great Let of the Wealth of this*
" *Land*. And the purvien of that *Act*, tended in the execu-
" tion contrary, EX DIAMETRO. *viz. To the high dis-*
pleasure of Almighty God, and the great Let, nay the utter
subversion of the common Law, and the great Let of the Wealth
of this Land, as hereafter shall appear: the substance of
which Act follows in these words.

THat from thenceforth, as well Justices of Assize, as
Justices of the Peace, in every County, upon information for the King, *before them made, without
any Finding or Presentment by Twelve men*, shall have full
Power and Authority, by their discretion ; and to hear and
determine all Offences, as Riots, unlawfull Assemblies, &c.
committed and done against any Act or Statute made, and
not repeal'd, &c. (*a case that very much resembles this of our
own times.*)

" By pretext of this Law, *Empson* and *Dudley* did commit
" upon the Subjects, unsufferable Pressure and Oppressions ;
" and therefore this Statute *was justly, soon after the decease of*
" Hen. *7. repealed*, at the next Parliament, after his decease,
" by the Statute of the 1 H. 8. chap. 6.

" *A good Caveat to Parliaments, to leave all causes to be*
" *measured by the Golden and Straight Metwand of the Law,*
" and not to the incertain and crooked Cord of discretion.

" It is almost incredible to foresee, when any *Maxime, or*
" *Fundamental Law, of this Realm is altered* (as elsewhere
" hath been observed) *what dangerous inconveniences do*
" *follow ;* which most expresly appeareth by this most unjust

" and strange Act of the eleventh of *H*. 7. For hereby, not only
" *Empson* and *Dudley* themselves, but such Justices of Peace
" (corrupt men) as they caused to be authorised, committed
" most grievous, and heavy Oppressions and Exactions; grind-
" ing the faces of the poor Subjects by penal Laws (be they
" never so obsolete, or unfit for the time) by information only,
" without any presentment, or tryal by Jury, being the an-
" tient Birth-right of the Subject ; but to hear and deter-
" mine the same, by their discretions; inflicting such penalty,
" as the Statute, not repealed, imposed.   These, and other
" like Oppressions and Exactions by, or by the means of
" *Empson* and *Dudley*, and their Instruments, brought
" infinite treasure to the Kings Cofers, whereof the King
" himself, at the end, with great grief, and compunction,
" repented, as in another place we have observed.

 " This Statute of the 11th of *H*. 7. we have receited, and
" shewed the just inconveniences thereof ; to the end that
" the like should never hereafter be attempted in any Court
" of Parliament ; and that others might avoid the fearful
" end of those two Time-servers, *Empson* and *Dudley, Qui*
" *eorum vestigiis insistunt, eorum exitus per horescant.*

 " See the Statute of 8 *Edw*. 4. chap. 2. a Statute of Liveries,
" an Information, &c.   By the discretion of the Judges,
" to stand as an Original, &c.   This Act is deservedly re-
" pealed, vide, 12 *R*. 2. chapter 13.   Punishment by dis-
" cretion &c. vide, 5th of *H*. 4. Chap. 6, 8. See the Commis-
" sion of Sewers ; discretion ought to be thus described,
" *Discretio est discernere per Legem, quid sit justum ;* From
" whence three things seem most remarkable.

 First, The great equity and justice of the great Charter,
with the high value our Ancestors have most deservedly set
upon it.

Secondly, The dreadful Maledictions, or Curse, they have denounced upon the Breakers of it ; with those exemplary punishments they have not spared to inflict upon such notorious Offenders.

Thirdly, So hainous a thing was it esteemed of old, to endeavour an enervation, or subversion of these Antient Rights and Priviledges, that Acts of Parliaments themselves (otherwise the most sacred with the People,) have not been of force enough to secure or defend such persons from condign punishment, who in pursuance of them, have acted inconsistant with our great *Charter*. Therefore it is, that that great Lawyer, the Lord *Cook*, doth more then once aggravate the example of *Empson* and *Dudley* (with persons of the same rank) into a just caution, as well to Parliaments as Judges, Justices as inferior Magistrates, to decline making, or executing any Act, that may in the least seem to restring or confirm this so often avowed and confirmed *Great Charter* of the Liberties of *England*, since Parliaments are said to err when they cross it ; the Obeyers of their Acts punished, as Time-serving Transgressors ; and that Kings themselves (though enriched by those courses) have with great Compunction and Repentance left among their dying words their Recantations.

Therefore most notable and true it was, with which we shall conclude this present Subject, what the King pleased to observe in a speech to the Parliament, about 1662. (*viz.*) *The good old Rules of Law are our best security.*

The manner of the *Courts* behaviour towards the Prisoners, and Jury, with their many extravigant Expressions, must not altogether slip our observation.

(1st) Their carriage to the *Jury* outdoes all presedents ; they entertained them more like a *Pack of Fellons*, then a

Jury of honest men, as being fitter to be try'd themselves, then to acquit others. In short, no Jury, for many Ages, received so many instances of displeasure and affront, *because they preferred not the humor of the Court before the quiet of their own Consciences, even to be esteemed as perjured, though they had really been so, had they not done what they did.*

(2d) Their treatment of the Prisoners was not more unchristian, than inhumane. History can scarce tell us of one *Heathen Roman* that ever was so ignoble to his Captive : What ! *to accuse, and not hear them ; to threaten to Bore their tongues, Gag and Stop their Mouths, Fetter their Leggs, meerly for defending themselves, and that by the antient fundamental Laws of* England *too.* O Barbarous ! had they been *Turks* and *Infidels*, that carriage would have ill become a Christian Court, *such actions proving much stronger disswasives, then Arguments to convince them, how much the Christian Religion inclines men to Justice and Moderation above their dark Idolatry.* It is truly lamentable that such occasion should be given, *for intelligence to Forreign Parts*, where *England* hath had the reputation of a Christian Country, *by the ill-treating of its sober and religious Inhabitants for their conscientious Meetings to worship God.* But, above all, *Dissenters* had little reason to have expected this boarish fierceness from the *Mayor* of *London, when they consider his eager prosecution of the Kings Party under* Cromwell's *Government, as thinking he could never give too great a Testimony of his Loyalty to that new Instrument*, which makes the old saying true, *That one Runagade is worse then three Turks.*

Alderman *Bloodworth*, being conscious to himself of his partial kindness to the *Popish Friars*, hopes to make amends by his zealous prosecution of the poor *Dissenters ;* for at the same Sessions he moved to have an Evidence (*of no small quality*) against *Harrisen,* the Mendicant Fryar, sent to *Bridewel* and whipt ; *he was earnest to have the Jury fined and imprisoned, because they brought not the Prisoners guilty, when no Crime was proved against them, but peaceably worshipping their God :* Whence it may be easie to observe, *That Popish Friars, and Prelatical Persecutors are meer Confederates.*

But what others have only adventured to stammer at, the Recorder of *London,* has been so ingenious as to speak most plainly ; or else, what means those two fatal Expressions, *which are become the talk and terror of City and Country ?*

First, in assuring the Jury, *That there would be a Law next Session of Parliament, That no man should have the protection of the Law, but such as conformed to the Church ;* which, should it be as true, as we hope it is false (and a dishonorable *Prophesie* of that great Assembly) *the* Papists *may live to see their* Marian *dayes out-done by profest Protestants.*

But surely no English-man can be so sottish, as to conceive that his right to *Liberty* and *Property,* came in with his Profession of the *Protestant Religion ;* or that his *natural and humane Rights, are dependant on certain Religious apprehensions ;* and consequently, he must esteem it a cruelty in the abstract, that Persons should be denied the benefit of those Laws which relate to civil concerns, who by their deportment in civil affairs, have no wayes transgrest them, but meerly upon an opinion of Faith, and matter of Conscience.

It is well known that *Liberty* and *Property, Trade* and *Commerce* were in the World long before the Points in difference betwixt *Protestants* and *Dissenters*, as the common Priviledges of Mankind ; and therefore not to be measured out by a conformity to this, or the other religious perswasion, but purely as *English-men.*

Secondly, But we should rather choose to esteem this an Expression of *heat* in the *Recorder*, then that we could believe a *Londons Recorder* should say, an *English Parliament* should impose so much *Slavery* on the present Age, and entayle it upon their own Posterity (*who for ought they know may be reckoned among the Dissenters of the next Age*) did he not encourage us to believe, it was both his *Desire* and his *Judgment*, from that deliberate *Elogy* he made on the *Spanish-Inquisition*, expressing himself much to this purpose : *viz.* " Till now I never understood the reason of the pollicy and " prudence of the *Spaniards*, in suffering the *Inquisition* " amongst them : And certainly it will never be well with " us, till some thing like unto the *Spanish Inquisition* be in " *England.*" The gross malignity of which saying, is almost inexpressable : *What does this but justifie that Hellish design of the Papists to have prevented the first Reformation ;* If this be good Doctrine, then *Hoggestrant*, the grand *Inquisitor*, was a more venerable Person then *Luther*, the Reformer. It was an expression that had better become *Cajetan* the *Popes Legate*, then *Howel*, a *Protestant Cities Recorder.* This is so far from helping to convert the *Spaniard*, that it is the way to *harden him in his Idolatry ;* when his abominable *cruelty* shall be esteemed prudence ; *and his most barbarous and exquisite torturing of Truth, an excellent way to prevent Faction.*

If the Recorder has spake for no more then for himself, it is well ; but certainly he little deserves to be thought a Protestant, *and a Lawyer, that puts both Reformation and Law into the Inquisition :* There being nothing more destructive of the fundamental Laws and Liberties of *England*, and that noble design of *primitive Reformation, then the Arbitrary Power and terrifying Raks of the Spanish Inquisition. And doubtless the* supream Governours of *the Land, are highly oblieged in* Honour *and* Conscience (in discharge of their Trust to God and the People, to take these things into their serious consideration, as what is expected from them, by those who earnestly wish their and the Kingdoms safety and prosperity.

A Postscript.

*The Copy of Judge Keeling's Case, taken
out of the Parliament Journal.*

Die Mercurij, 11th Decembris, 1667.

THe House resumed the Hearing of the rest of the Report touching the matter of Restraints upon Juries ; and that upon the examination of divers Witnesses, in several Clauses of restraints, put upon Juries, by the Lord Chief Justice Keeling ; whereupon the Committee made their Resolutions, which are as followeth.

First, *That the proceedings of the Lord Chief Justice, in the Cases now reported, are Innovations, in the Trial of men for their Lives and Liberties ; and that he hath used an Arbitrary and Illegal power, which is of dangerous consequence to the Lives and Jiberties of the people of* England, *and tends to the introducing of an Arbitrary Government.*

Secondly, *That in the place of Judicature, the Lord Chief Justice hath under-valued, vilified, and contemned* Magna Charta, *the great Preservers of our Lives, Freedom, and Property.*

Thirdly, *That he be brought to Trial, in order to condign punishment, in such manner as the House should judge most fit and requisite.*

Die Veneris, 13th Decembris, 1667.

Resolved, &c.

That the Presedents and Practise of Fining or Imprisoning, Jurors, for Verdicts, is Illegal.

Now whether the Justices of this Court, in their Proceedings (both towards the Prisoners, and Jury) have acted according to Law, to their Oaths and Duty, and to do Justice without partiality, whereby Right might be preserved, the Peace of the Land secured, and our Ancient Laws established or whether such actions tend not to deprive as of our Lives and Liberties to rob us of (our Birth-right) the Fundamental Laws of *England*, and finally to bring in an Arbitrary and Illegal power to usurp the Benches of all our Courts of Justice we leave the *English* Reader to judge?

Certainly, there can be no higher affront offered to King and Parliament, then the bringing their Reputations into suspition with their People by the irregular actions of subordinate Judges : And no Age can parallel the carriage of this *Recorder*, *Mayor*, &c. Nor can we think so ignobly of the Parliament, as that they should do less then call these Persons to account, who fail'd not to do it to one less guilty, and of more repute (to wit), Judge *Keeling* : For if his behaviour gave just ground of jealousie, that he intended an Innovation, and the introducing an Arbitrary Government, this *Recorder* much more. Did chief Justice *Keeling* say, *Magna Charta* was *Magna farta* ; so did this *Recorder* too : And did Justice *Keeling* Fine and Imprison Juries, contrary to all Law, so did this *Recorder* also. In short, there is no difference, unless it be, that the one was questioned, and the other deserves it : But we desire in this they may be said to differ, That though the former escap'd punishment, the latter may not, who having a Presedent before did notwithstanding notoriously transgress.

To conclude, The Law supposes the King can't err, because it is willing to suppose, he alwayes acts by Law (and *Voluntas Legis, est voluntas Regis,* Or the Kings Will is regulated by the Law) but it says no such thing of his Judges. And since they are oblig'd by Oath to disregard the Kings Letters (though under the Broad and privy-Seal) if they any wise oppugn, or contradict the Laws of the Land ; and considering that every singular Action of an inferior Minister, has an ugly reference to the Supream Magistrate, where not rebuked ; we can't but conclude, that both Judges are answerable for their irregularities, especially, where they had not a limitation of a Kings Letter, or Command ; and that the Supream Magistrate is oblig'd, as in Honour and Safety to himself, *Alfred*-like, to bring such to condign punishment, lest every Sessions produce the like Tragical Scenes of Usurpation over the Consciences of Juries, to the villifying and contemning of Justice, and great detriment, and prejudice of the good and honest men of this Famous and Free City.

FIAT JUSTICIA.

FINIS.

Milton Keynes UK
Ingram Content Group UK Ltd.
UKHW020657080324
439098UK00005B/285